Jean.

In this season of
Spirit your sparkle
adds a touch of jolly -
which began in September
and continues through
winter bitterness -
Spring will find a
new robin to sing
happily. For this
I am happy.

L.

DEDICATED TO

MY BELOVED FRIEND

AND TEACHER

Hoga Fujiwara

ILLUSTRATED BY GRISHA DOTZENKO

NINA CLARK POWELL

Japanese Flower Arrangement

FOR BEGINNERS

CHARLES SCRIBNER'S SONS NEW YORK

A–1.62 [MH]

Printed in the United States of America
Library of Congress Catalog Card Number 62-7148

Foreword

Interest in and appreciation of Japanese flower arranging—Ikebana—has spread throughout the United States in recent years. The need for basic instructions for the beginner in Japanese flower arranging has grown with this increase in interest. Nina Powell, Professor of the Ohara School of Flower Arrangement, has recognized this need. In this book for the beginner, she presents a sound foundation in techniques, concepts and Moribana styles of arrangements as they are taught by the Ohara School.

Mrs. Powell studied both modern and classical schools of Ikebana during her two years in Japan. However, she concentrated on the Ohara School, because she felt it provided the most suitable styles of arrangements for American homes. Nina Powell hoped to teach flower arrangement upon her return to the United States. She believed that American women would be interested in learning the art of Ikebana if the chance were offered to them. Her hopes have been confirmed. In the three years since her return to the United States, she has taught constantly—both at the University of New Mexico Community College and a number of small private classes.

This book contains suggestions as to plant materials suitable for the various styles of arrangements. The step-by-step instructions for Ohara School Moribana arrangements are clear and easy to follow. Nina Powell's book makes successful Japanese arrangements possible for the beginning arranger.

I am delighted to commend this book by a teacher of the Ohara School to all who would learn Japanese flower arranging.

HOUN OHARA
Head Master of the
Ohara School of Ikebana

Contents

General Information

FLOWER ARRANGEMENT is one of many artistic pursuits of the Japanese people. All of their artistic endeavors are interrelated by means of basic principles of art. They feel that through the creative use of natural materials they develop spiritual as well as material life. They constantly aspire to harmony between their natural and spiritual worlds.

Ikebana, the Japanese word for flower arrangement, means not only flower arrangement, but includes the materials used in the arrangement as well. Materials which may be used in flower arranging are dried materials, seed pods, leaves and branches, evergreens, flowers, shrubs, trees and vines, berries and fruits, stones, wooden shapes and woven goods. In fact, the materials and their use are limited only by the imagination of the arranger.

The Tokonoma, which has evolved from the "Oshi-ita," has been for many centuries the focal point of the Japanese room. It is a recessed niche some two to three feet in depth with its platform raised about six inches above the level of the floor. The Tokonoma will usually measure two to four feet in width and some four to six feet in height; however, its measurements are determined by the proportions of the room.

The flower arrangement is placed on the floor of the Tokonoma, either to the right or to the left side. An incense burner, or similar art object, goes in the center of the area. A scroll is usually hung in the back of the Tokonoma. Encompassed within the walls of the Tokonoma these three items make a complete setting and thereby create an harmonious whole.

Flower arrangement is intimately tied to Japanese religions. The most ancient faith is Shinto. Many myths relate the gods to flowers. Even today on New Year's Day, when a new home is built—or for that matter almost any structure—Shinto rites are held. Placed before the structure one will find pine and bamboo bound together with little white prayer cards hanging from the sheaf to ward off evil spirits and to bring down blessings on the endeavor. While the Shinto worship was simple and naturalistic, it did not satisfy the Buddhist thirst for color.

The Buddhist faith came to Japan in the sixth century. It was brought back as part of the cultural background of China by envoys of the Japanese court who had been sent to China to study. The Prince Regent of Japan, Shataku Taishu, sent many educated noblemen to China to learn about the Chinese civilization in order that the knowledge would serve to advance the culture of Japan.

Many of these men spent most of their lives in China learning of that country's arts and people and returned home in old age as sages of the court.

The teachings of Buddha were accepted by many of these men and they returned to Japan teaching this new ideology. For several centuries Buddhism was confined to the noble and scholar. The priests were kept by the State and had time to study and to teach the new concepts. The Buddhist ritual and ceremony were ideally suited to court life. The first form of Buddhist flower arrangement came from simply throwing flower petals in the paths of processions. The idea of colorful flowers appealed to the Japanese, but not the wilful destruction of plant life—and so live flower arrangements were developed.

The first great master of Ikebana was Ono-no-imoko, one of the envoys of the Prince Regent. After serving his master until his death, Ono-no-imoko retired from court life, built himself a small house by a lake near Kyoto and spent his days in praying for his deceased master and developing the basic style of flower arrangement which we know as Rikkwa.

After he had developed his art others came to learn. Those followers named their master Ikenobo, which means "hermit by the lake." Thus came into being the first school of Ikebana—Ikenobo.

The Ikenobo School of Ikebana was perpetuated by the Buddhist priests, noblemen and the members of Ono-no-imoko's family. In the fourteenth century the first treatise was written on the Rikkwa form. Yoshimasa, one of the Ashikaga rulers and a patron of the arts, recognized the beauty of flower arrangements and publicly acclaimed the Ikenobo School.

Toward the end of the fifteenth century, Ikenobo had developed the Shoka or Seika style as we know it today along the lines of the "heaven, earth and man" concept. So-ami, a tea master and companion of Yoshimasa, was the first to symbolize spiritual truths through flowers. He gave the following definitions to the three principal stems:

Heaven — encompasses all of the elements.
Man — makes life active.
Earth — gives form to all life.

So-ami used the Chinese Buddhist concept of Ten Chi Jin. This concept was first used in Chinese paintings and means that each work of art must have an outstanding subject, a helper or secondary feature which supports the subject and a smaller object or group of helpers to fill out the composition.

Today all Japanese schools of flower arrangement use the art principles of the three branches but many schools have substituted new names. Some of these names reflect nationalistic and internationalistic trends while others hold to classic Japanese words.

School	*Heaven*	*Man*	*Earth*
Ohara	Subject	Secondary	Object
Ikenobo	Shin	Soe	Tai
Kofu	Shin	Soe	Tome
Sho-fu-ryu	Shin	Soe	Tai
Sogetsu	Shin	Soe	Hikae
Modern	Tenno (Emperor)	Chichihaha (Father-Mother)	Kodomo (Children)

Ikebana has held the same prestige artistically as sand-painting, the tea ceremony and incense burning. It started as a religious and aesthetic pleasure of the priests and nobility. However, by the fourteenth century the art of flower arrangement had permeated the homes of the Japanese people.

The door was opened by the way of religious festivals and worship. The religious significance of flower arrangements placed in the Buddhist temples and Shinto shrines leaves little doubt as to the devotion of the Japanese for their ancestors, nature and beauty.

At home an arrangement may be a single flower, two or three twigs or a large and elegant arrangement; but it is always there. The Japanese housewife shops for flowers when she shops for food, which is daily. She attends a weekly class for study and arrangement, when she can afford it, meeting with friends, neighbors and her teacher to improve her art.

On entering a Japanese room, etiquette requires that you admire first the art of the arranger, then the plant material, then the Kakemono (scroll) which is hung above the arrangement in the Tokonoma.

Types of Arrangements

Traditional arrangements are divided into two basic groups. These two groups are classical and naturalistic. The classical group is composed of *Rikkwa* and *Seika*, while the naturalistic group is subdivided into *Moribana* and *Heika* or *Nageire*.

Ikenobo stands as the venerable grandfather of flower arrangement schools. His children are many and have sprung up all over Japan since World War II as though to satisfy the insatiable curiosity of Americans who want to learn. I shall list only those types of arrangements which have already established reputations for age and art.

Rikkwa is a classical arrangement of standing plant materials. It was developed for altar arrangements and depicted the whole of nature from streams to mountains. It was large, stiff and very formal. These arrangements are rarely seen today as they take days and many knowing hands to create. Each flower and stem in the arrangement is carefully taped, wired and wrapped to fit its place in the whole composition. Rikkwa was perfected by the Ikenobo School in Kyoto.

Seika is a formalized treatment of line using fresh flowers or branches. Three points of the triangle or crescent are always clearly in evidence. Seika style has remained practically unchanged for the last five hundred years, and is used today as much as the more modern styles.

Tsuribana is suspended flowers, usually in a basket.

Kakebana is flowers hanging from the wall. These arrangements often use baskets, bamboo stems, art objects and ceramic bowls fastened to the wall as their containers. They are light and delicate. Vines and bare branches emphasize line.

Chabana is the traditional Tea Ceremony arrangement. The style was developed in the sixteenth century to depict nature. The arrangements are simple—often only one flower with its own leaves. It was developed as an expression of the Zen Sect of Buddhism. Its purpose was to aid in meditating the beauty of nature.

Nageire originally meant "thrown-in flowers." It is arranged in a tall vase and has a free, natural appearance. Thus Nageire and Heika are more or less interchangeable terms; however, Nageire strives to express the natural growth of plant material emphasizing line.

Heika was developed in the twelfth century. Heika arrangements follow along the lines of the ancient Rikkwa, but are much simpler. Literally Heika means "tall vase." They are naturalistic and informal.

Moribana means "piled up" flowers in a low bowl. It depicts nature but allows greater freedom in arranging than did previous forms of arrangements.

Free Style is a modern development. A Free Style arrangement is a creative work of art based on the knowledge, skill and imagination of the disciplined arranger. It allows free use of any material which suits the purpose of the design.

Morimono consists of arranging fruits, flowers, branches and stones together in flat bowls, baskets or plates.

Modern Schools

Today there are thousands of teachers of flower arrangement in Japan, and hundreds of schools throughout the islands. About one hundred of these schools are recognized by the Japanese Board of Education. The large cities have representation of both modern and classical schools while small towns and villages cling to the classical styles.

Anyone can originate and teach a new school —if he or she can get a following; but to be recognized one must pass examinations given by the Board of Education. It is a fact, however, that all of the great teachers have been men. Each school sets up exhibits in which students must participate in order to acquire points necessary for promotion, but there is no competition as we know it in our flower shows.

These are some of the present-day schools which enjoy great popularity: Kofu, Koryu, Shofu-ryu, Enshui-ryu, Shoka, Yamato, Kokufu, Saga, Misho, Ikanega and Ikenobo. Most of these schools teach the Seika styles in formal, semi-formal and informal techniques of Ikenobo as a fundamental of Ikebana. They also teach the Moribana and more abstract types of arrangemens—the free styles.

The two most ambitious modern schools are *Sogetsu* and *Ohara*. These schools base their teachings on the traditional Ikenobo; but they have tried to adapt their teachings to fit modern life in all its aspects. Through them flower arranging has become truly universal—in composition, expression and spirit.

Ohara School

The Ohara School is the basic source for the lessons in this book. It was founded by Unshin Ohara, grandfather of the present Master Houn Ohara. Unshin Ohara was originator of the Moribana style about fifty years ago. At the time his problems were many—a break with tradition, suitable containers to work with and the disapproval of his fellow masters. Today, however, we reap the benefits of his efforts—a beautiful style of flower arrangements and new ceramics adaptable to our needs.

Houn Ohara has continued the work of his grandfather and father Koun Ohara and is internationally famous for his flower arrangements. He is also well known for his creative artistry in ceramics.

The school teaches two basic methods of arrangement—*Moribana* or low bowl, and *Heika* or tall vase. There are the usual rules of preparation, materials, position and so forth; but there is also included ample room for the play of creative imagination.

For each method—Moribana and Heika—there are five basic styles of arrangements, each giving a different effect and expression in the completed composition. The five styles are: UPRIGHT, SLANTING or WATER-REFLECTING, CASCADE, HEAVENLY and CONTRASTING.

As one masters the techniques of the basic Moribana and Heika methods, the way is opened for more creative interpretations of materials such as the VARIATIONS and FREE STYLES.

The Ohara School divides these basic arrangements into five types:

1. *Naturalistic.* This type is an expression of nature. All lines do not have to follow the basic directions. Overcrossed lines indicate life and movement, such as a broken wheat stalk brushed by a bird's wing. The bent line must be in proportion with the remainder of the arrangement before it is bent.

2. *Color Scheme.* This places strong emphasis on color and form.

3. *Mass Technique.* This method plays up force and volume by working with flowers as groups rather than singly, and need not represent them as they grow in nature.

4. *Thin Lines.* Such arrangements are made with reeds, cattails, peeled wisteria and similar materials which have strong lines. These arrangements express rhythmic forms and geometric designs.

5. *Not Using Flowers.* Materials used in these arrangements can include such things as rope, stone, glass, shrubs, dried wood, metal, etc. It is considered the avant garde type of flower arranging and is not suitable for beginners to try. It is usually several years before a Japanese student will venture into this type of arranging.

Trends in the Ohara School

The present-day trend shows up as either *Realistic* or *Non-Realistic*. Our purpose here is to work with realistic materials and arrangements. These are the familiar flowers, shrubs, trees, dried materials, etc. Used to create basic styles of Moribana in familiar forms, these provide us with realistic arrangements. The non-realistic trends take us into the realm of symbolism. This form of styling makes use of plant material, bowls, stones, sculpture, art objects and, in fact, anything suitable to the mind of the creator, to produce what would be called an abstract work of art in painting. Here color, shape and texture are more important than realistic or natural beauty.

Color

The Japanese do not use a color chart. To them, color lends interest to an arrangement and sometimes a focal point, but primarily they are interested in their material being used together harmoniously to make a pleasing arrangement, rather than depending upon the shading of colors to produce the desired effects. Part of the need for a color scheme is eliminated by the use of shrubs, vines, evergreens and trees as a background for basically two colors of fresh flower materials.

TOOLS FOR FLOWER ARRANGING

Bowls. These are the first necessity for flower arrangements. Since we are working with only Moribana arrangements, our bowls must be low with wide mouths. The bowl you use has several purposes to fulfil. As a part of the arrangement it must blend with the arrangement and be in proportion with it. Its shape is important, with the sides low enough to provide ample hand working room. The bowl should blend with the setting in which it will be used.

Beginners in the Ohara School in Japan use a standard circular white bowl about fifteen inches across with two-inch sides. Any similar bowl will amply serve the purpose. Colors of pottery bowls are quiet and subdued—grey, tan and black are great favorites.

Needlepoint Holders. These come in various sizes and shapes. I find that a 2 × 3″ rectangle or oval will serve quite adequately. It is advisable to buy your holders to suit a specific type of bowl. Also, think in terms of the weight of plant materials you plan to use. Heavy materials demand heavy needlepoint holders.

Scissors. These are available in various types. My choice is small pruning shears. A short knife and saw are indispensable for large arrangements using thick branches.

Wire, Clay and Florist Tape. Aids such as these are not often used in Japan as the designs and materials do not need them. The Japanese make an arrangement in the setting where it is to be viewed. However, these aids are recommended for inclusion as a part of your work kit. When moving finished arrangements about the house, clay is indispensable to hold the work in place.

Rice straw is the Japanese substitute for wire. The florists use it to tie up the bunches of flowers when they are sold. As with the straw, the arranger should make use of wire if needed to hold the arrangement together—making sure that the wire is kept out of sight.

Materials for Basic Arrangements

Three types of materials are preferable for

beginner's arrangements. However, if necessary, two are permissible.

The Subject and Secondary stems should be branches of trees or shrubs, either deciduous or evergreen. Interesting seed pods, leaves, fruits and flowers are also usable. The Object stem, or group, should be composed of flowers. These flowers should be fairly large and imposing. If possible, pick one in full bloom, one in bud, etc. The intermediaries should be soft in texture and can be either green or flowers. Cushion or azalea mums are lovely fillers with many fall flowers if their color is in harmony with the other materials. Green and dried grasses, fern and pine make interesting fillers.

Rules and Techniques for Moribana

Before we can actually make a Japanese arrangement it will be necessary to discuss a few rules of mechanics. In this chapter we will study the basic techniques and materials which apply to all five styles of Moribana arrangements. We cannot hope to cover all of the information which you will need but this will give you a foundation of basic information on which to build.

The favorite containers of the Japanese, beside baskets, are made of copper, bronze and pottery. They feel that simple ceramic containers display the natural beauty of plants to better advantage than do elaborate and distracting vases. For large and heavy arrangements massive bronze and copper containers are used.

In this course, pottery, glass, copper, brass and bronze bowls or vases are all suitable. Use what you have. We especially want your arrangements to fit your home. The only requirement is that the finished arrangement be in proportion with the container and in harmony with its setting. Needlepoint holders are always covered in the finished arrangement. This is especially important in Moribana styles as the open-mouthed bowls leave a clear view of the base of your work. Moss was a common cover in earlier Japanese days but as it is not readily available today we must resort to local materials. Leaves from the plants we are using, marbles and native stones will serve adequately to cover the needlepoint holder and at the same time give a finished look to the arrange ment.

Stands and bases serve a practical as well as aesthetic purpose. They protect your tabletops from scratches and water marks. They define the limits of your arrangement and they can be chosen to add height and color to your arrangement. Any material which will suitably complete your arrangement is satisfactory. However, the Japanese love the large polished slabs of native wood for their naturalistic arrangements. They use the carved lacquered stands for their brass, bronze and copper bowls, and reed and bamboo mats for rough pottery and lacquerware. They usually use a square base for a round container and vice versa.

In this book you will attain general background in Japanese flower arranging and specific instruction in the Ohara School Moribana styles. As the Ohara School teaches two basic methods perhaps it is wise to clarify the differences.

The primary distinction between the Moribana and Heika arrangement is technique. Moribana uses a needlepoint holder in a flat bowl whereas Heika uses braces attached to the main branches in a tall vase. Some of the modern vases can be used with either style.

As a beginner in Ikebana you should not let yourself become discouraged by the number of rules or subtleties of flower arranging. During the first two and one-half years of study in the Ohara School all materials used by the student are those chosen by the teacher. After this initial period the student is then free to choose her own materials. The idea is that the student must learn intuitively the purpose behind the teacher's choice as well as proportion and balance for many materials. After she has done this, she is ready to proceed to more difficult work. Sometimes a student will repeat an arrangement many times before her teacher approves it.

Protecting Bowls and Vases

Silver containers will not tarnish or be scratched if a piece of aluminum foil is wrapped around the needlepoint holder or is placed beneath it.

Crystal can be protected in the same manner and the foil will add to the appearance of the bottom of the vase.

Ceramic bowls can be protected from scratches by placing a small square of paper under the needlepoint holder. Baskets can be protected by attaching the holder with a piece of clay.

Mexican and Indian Pottery is best suited for dried arrangements. If they must be used for fresh arrangements be sure to use a glass, jar or can to hold the water. Even the new varnish and plastic sprays do not protect them from seepage and water stains.

Mineral Deposits can be removed from your bowls with commercial products.

Water will not splash when poured into a vase if it is poured onto the needlepoint holder.

Symbols for Sketches

There is a symbolic theory which states that Heaven (male) is round and Earth (female) is square, and all things born of the two (man) form a triangle. These symbols are not used today in the Ohara School, but I find that they simplify understanding any sketched arrangement, so we shall use them.

Heaven is male — ○ — and is referred to as the Subject Stem.

Man is the combination — △ — and is referred to as the Secondary Stem.

Earth is female — □ — and is referred to as the Object Stem.

Intermediaries (fillers) are shown as: ⊤

The fact that the Navaho Indians have always used the ○ to denote male and the □ to

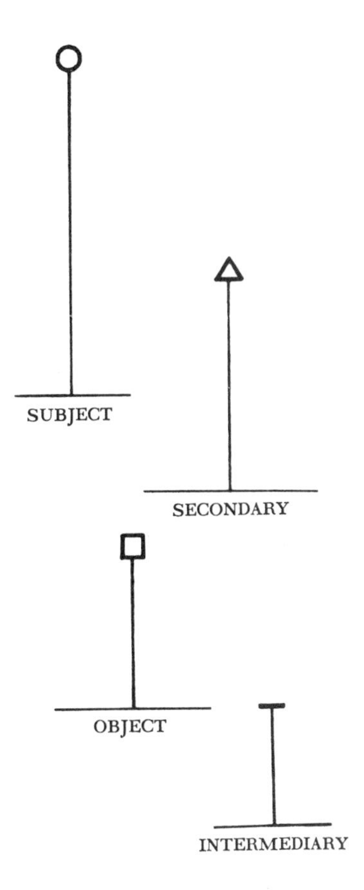

denote female gives us some idea of the antiquity of the symbols.

BASIC STYLE DESIGNS

All Moribana arrangements are based on a scalene triangle. They are made to be viewed from a sitting position with the arrangement a little below eye level. As there is only one best position from which to view the finished arrangement, it is always best to choose a style most adapted to the location in which you plan to put your finished arrangement. Ideally it will be viewed from a distance of five or six feet. Imagine yourself in that position and the sketches below will help you visualize the outlines of the five styles of Moribana which will be studied.

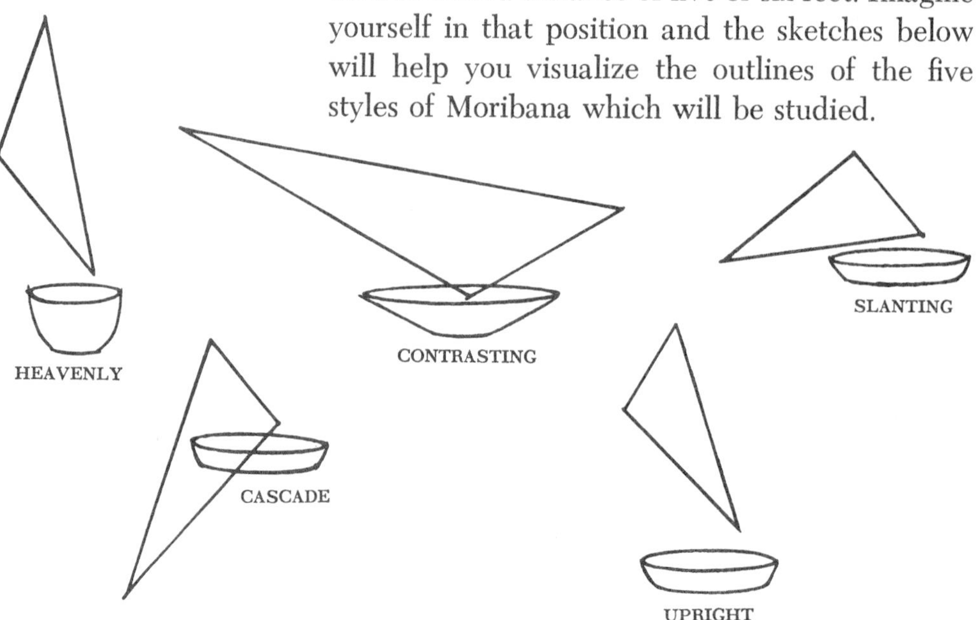

Measurements for Various Sizes of Containers

Lengths of the principal stems normally vary according to the container used. Sometimes they are varied in accordance with the nature of the material and that style of the arrangement. In general, however, the basic measurements for Moribana and Heika are fixed—though they are not absolute in application.

SMALL

Subject	Length plus depth of container	1½ length plus container depth	Twice the length plus depth of container
Secondary	⅔ Subject	⅔ Subject	⅔ Subject
Object	½ Subject	½ Subject	½ Subject

MEDIUM

The above rules are intended to be used as a guide in making the Upright, Contrasting, Slanting and Water-Reflecting styles of arrangements.

In arrangements of the heavenly and cascade styles the basic measurements are as follows:

Subject — more than twice the width plus the depth of the container.

Secondary — one-half the length of the Subject Stem.

Object — one-third the length of the Subject Stem.

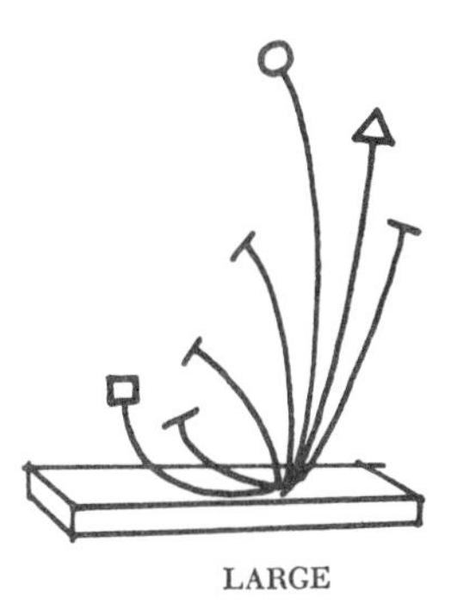
LARGE

Stem measurements are taken from below

the head of the last blossom, especially with flowers like gladiolus, lilies and bell flowers. In the case of the intermediaries such as gypsophila and similar small flowers on delicate stems, the heads can be considered part of the total measurement.

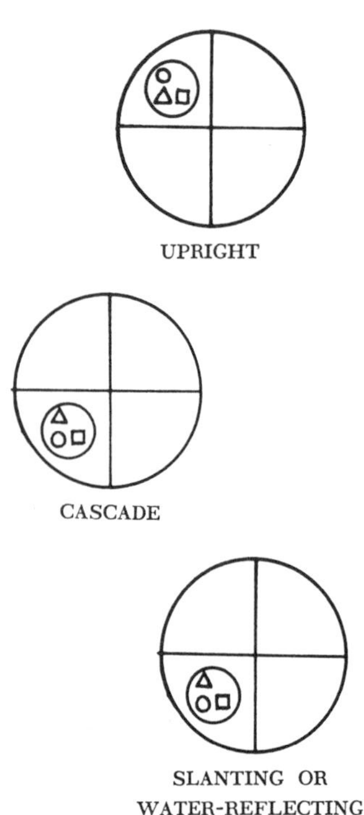

Positioning Holders and Stems

The positions of the needlepoint holder in the container change according to the style of arrangement you are making. The sketches at the left show locations for left-hand placements. A mirror image of these will give you the right-hand placement for an arrangement. You have the choice of left- or right-hand placement for your arrangement but you cannot move from the back to the front of the container.

In Upright, Cascade and Slanting (or Water-Reflecting) styles of arrangement your flowers will be placed on the needlepoint holder in a triangle if you look down into the bowl. Look at the needlepoint holder and visually divide it into a triangle with the narrow point coming toward you. The style of the arrangement will determine the placement of the three main stems on the points of the triangle. The chapters on specific styles will contain the details for this placement of the stems.

In the Heavenly and Contrasting styles we work from the center of the bowl and the above rules do not apply. In Heavenly styles the three main stems march down the center of the needle-point holder "soldier fashion" and start forming their triangle by angles above the holder. This is shown in the sketch at the right.

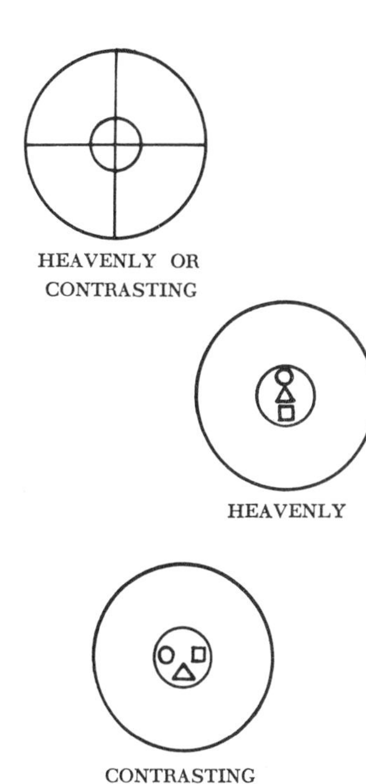

In the Contrasting style the needlepoint holder is again placed in the center of the bowl and toward the front edge if desired. The Subject and Secondary stems are placed so that they go out in opposite directions but appear to be growing from one root. The Object stem comes forward in the center. This triangle is completely in front of the container using the front half of the bowl.

Positions of Heads of Flowers

In all arrangements and styles always point the heads up, or toward you and up. One easy way to remember how to place the flowers is to imagine that you, the arranger, are the sun, and the lush growth is toward you. The back of the arrangement would be North, and plants to the back of the finished arrangement would be smaller and of slower growth. Never allow flower heads to droop, unless you are using a flower such as wisteria which droops naturally.

Grooming

Basically this is done by first removing all leaves which might go into the water. Pine branches are easiest to clean thoroughly if the needles are picked off. Cutting them results in a ragged appearance. Remove all unsightly dead twigs. If in doubt as to the number of leaves to remove, wait until you have finished your arrangement. Place your hand over a leaf or branch in question. If the composition is good without that leaf or branch, then remove it.

If the branch is heavy and twiggy, remove leaves alternately from opposite sides. Also remove branches if they interfere with the clean line desired.

When arranging flowers with clusters of blossoms, remove all dead and old ones. Often a single small flower on a stem can be more charming than a cluster and gives a cleaner line.

Care and Preservation of Plant Material

cutting and hardening

1. Always cut plant material at least four and preferably eight hours before arranging. Morning before the sun hits the plants, and late afternoon, after they have stored food for the day, are the best times for cutting.

2. Cut stems on an angle and strip off all leaves which will rest in the water.

3. Carry a pail half-filled with water when you go into the garden to cut flowers. Place the flowers in the pail as soon as they have been cut.

4. When you have finished cutting, fill the pail until only the heads of the flowers remain exposed above the water.

5. Place the pail of flowers in a cool place until you are ready to use the flowers for arrangements.

6. Any plant which oozes a milky substance should be charred as soon as it is cut and then placed in the water. This applies to poinsettias, dahlias and poppies.

7. Roses, lilacs and chrysanthemums can be dipped in boiling water for about one minute to preserve them. Only about an inch of the stem needs to be treated. Carefully wrap the blooms with paper to keep them from being scalded by the steam.

8. When arranging roses, chrysanthemums, lilacs and other woody stems, it will aid in preserving the blooms if you will crush the bottom of the stem for a half-inch.

9. Cutting the stems under water when arranging will keep them from getting air pockets at the base.

10. To slow the opening process of tulips, their stems can be dipped in sugar or placed in a sugar solution, or sugar can be placed on the holder. The petals can be rubbed with a bit of egg white, then pressed gently together and they will not open.

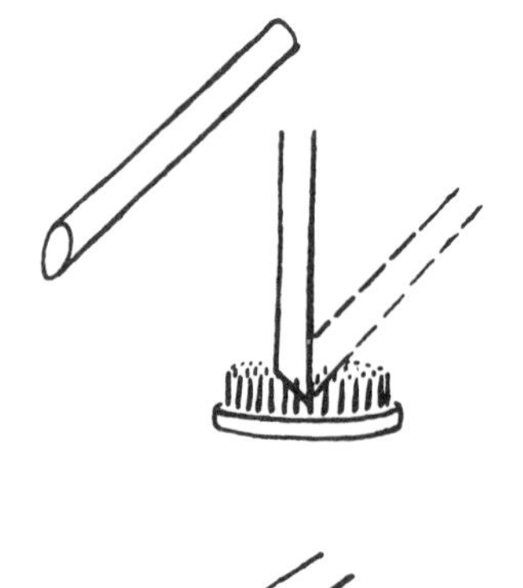

11. Gladiolus will open faster when placed in warm water. The bloom opening process can be retarded by placing the flowers in the refrigerator.

12. When placing stems on the needlepoint holder, cut them at an angle and then anchor the stem so that the short side is up. Placing stems in this manner provides a larger area for the absorption of water and will aid in keeping the flowers fresh longer.

13. When branches are difficult to bend, they can be notched on the side away from the bend. This will make them easier to shape and less liable to break.

14. To brace top-heavy stems, place small lengths of stem in front or back of the heavy stem as necessary.

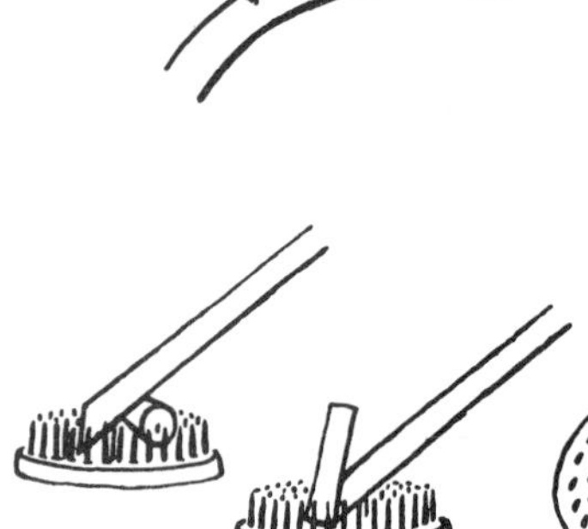

15. While the above rules apply to most of the plants in your garden, the hardening treatment for bamboo is as outlined below.

Cut the bamboo at sunrise or at sunset.

Make a hole through the first joint. A small nail will do this job nicely. Make a solution of ½ teaspoon alcohol, ½ teaspoon peppermint oil and 1 cup of water. Shake well. If the hole is too small for pouring, an eye dropper can be used to force the solution into the joint.

16. The aforementioned solution of alcohol and peppermint oil will harden roses when the stems are immersed one to two inches in the solution for about three minutes. This treatment for roses works better than any others I have tried.

17. When cutting off a branch large enough to leave a scar, touch it up with stain, cigarette ash, ink or paint; or see that a twig from another branch covers and hides the scar.

STRENGTHENING STEMS

To strengthen stems of vines and weak flowers, the following methods may be used:

1. Wire a stronger stem to the weaker one as high up the branch as necessary, and insert on the holder as one.

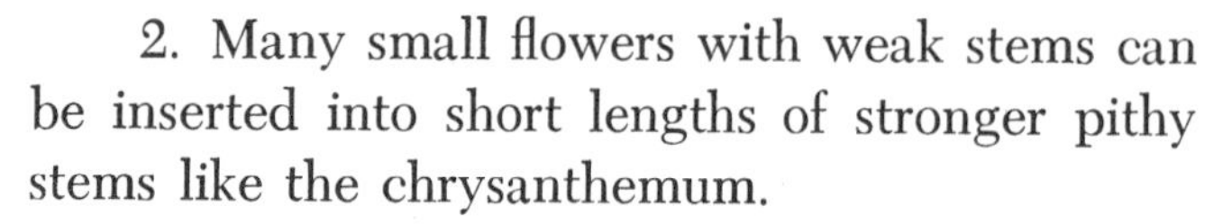

2. Many small flowers with weak stems can be inserted into short lengths of stronger pithy stems like the chrysanthemum.

3. Hollow-stemmed plants like lotus, onions, waterlilies and amaryllis should first have water forced into the flower with a syringe. Then a firm stem such as the chrysanthemum should be forced up into the flower stalk before attempting to use it in an arrangement. Unless they are strengthened, the hollow-stemmed plants will peel or break and fall over.

4. Small stems can be wrapped in tissue paper if other branches are not available for strengthening them.

WATERING

Once the arrangement is finished, it will last longer if the water is changed daily. A small syringe is ideal for removing the water from the bowl, as this leaves the arrangement undisturbed. The water level should be kept at least one inch high.

Pussy Willow Branches

Pussy willow branches are especially good for small arrangements using two or three flowers.

To clean husks from pussy willow, press gently with the thumbnail at the base of the catkin. The husk will crack or tear. Carefully remove husk. Once the husk is removed, the silky catkins swell.

To bend pussy willow branches to the desired shape, grip them firmly with both hands. Hold with thumbs together on the underside of the curve. Gently and slowly work hands up the branch—with firm pressure on bend between thumbs. If you desire more curve than you can get the first time, repeat the process. If you are using several branches, bend all of them to suit you before trying to arrange them.

Large Branches and Driftwood

When using large branches of driftwood or fresh material, your work is often easier if you prepare the large branches separately from the other arrangement materials.

1. Determine the length and angle desired for the branch, and cut to suit.

2. Either nail or screw the branch onto a board which will fit inside the bowl. Be careful to see that the branch will balance on its wooden base.

3. Place the branch and board in position. Place the needlepoint holder close to the branch on the board and continue making the arrangement in the usual manner.

4. When the arrangement is finished, cover the board with rocks or pebbles to imitate nature.

5. Sand or small pebbles can be used to cover the base and needlepoint holder of arrangements using all dried materials. They can also be used as a base accessory for the total arrangement. Often, by properly shaping the sand or pea gravel, it is possible to emphasize the line of the container or the effectiveness of a line or mass arrangement.

Morning Glories

This material must be hardened in water for a period of four to eight hours prior to use. Cut vines with many unopened buds, cutting carefully to obtain lengths you expect to use. Remove open flowers and dead ones before you make your arrangement. Place full buds in key positions. The finished arrangement can be kept fresh by snipping off the dead blooms. Such an arrangement will last several days. Morning glories are most suited to baskets and hanging containers.

Upright Style

MATERIALS: Forsythia and Tulips
BOWL: Green glaze—12×10×2″

PLACE needlepoint holder in the back right-hand quarter of the bowl. Check plant material for the longest and strongest stem. Measure it in relation to your bowl and cut it to the correct length. Choose the second strongest stem and cut it ⅔ the length of the first stem. Choose your nicest open flower and cut it ½ the length of the first stem. These are the materials for the triangle of your arrangement. Any other materials which you add will be called intermediaries. You are not limited as to the number of these intermediaries.

The longest stem is your Subject. It is placed on the back right-hand corner of your needlepoint holder. Force it straight down on the holder and slant it back slightly. If the branch has a natural curve, place the stem so that the point turns in over the center of the bowl.

The second longest stem is your Secondary. It is placed to the right and in front of the Subject stem. It is angled forward and out to the right, extending beyond the edge of the bowl. If there is a curve to the stem it should follow the line of the Subject stem toward the center of the bowl.

The third stem, or Object, is placed straight up on the holder on the left-hand front corner and angled out to the left front, extending over the edge of the bowl in front.

If the branches are thin and intermediaries are needed, they are cut various lengths to fill gaps. The fillers are always shorter than the main stem which they complement.

In placing your intermediaries, or fillers, it is good to think in terms of three. The main stem and two fillers is an example of this. If you are using pine for your Subject and Secondary stems, you should use pine for the intermediaries. If you are using roses for your Object group, you should use roses for your intermediaries. A second group of flowers can be introduced, however, if they are used in such a way as to complement the Object group.

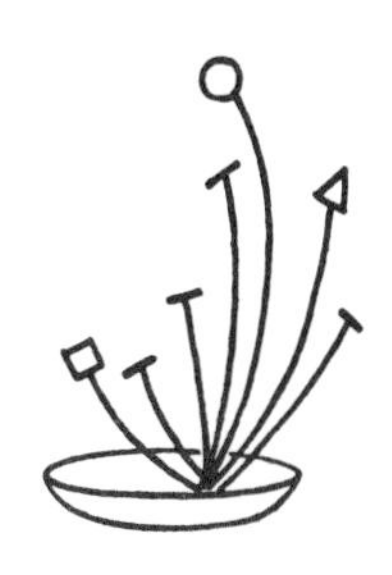

OUTLINE OF THE THREE MAIN STEMS WITH FOUR INTERMEDIARIES

Plant Material Suitable for the Upright Style

Dogwood
Redbud
Red oak
Pinyon pine
Ponderosa pine
White pine
Rhododendron
Swamp magnolia
Bare, budded or seeded branches of:

- Maple
- Horse chestnut
- Mulberry
- Poplar
- Elm

Pussy willow
Lilac
Nandina
Cane
Bamboo
Reeds
Ligustrum
Photinia
Cattails
Pampas grass
Mahonia

Driftwood
Hydrangea
Raspberry branches
Hemlock
Eucalyptus
Japanese yew
Barberry
Mock orange
Loquat
Amaryllis
Flowering almond
Cottonwood with flowers
Wheat
Wild grasses
Scotch broom
Azalea
Camellia
Canna lilies
Delphinium
Buddleia
Tulips
Water lilies
Peonies
Snowball
Pyracantha

Trees with seed pods
- Sycamore
- Persimmon

Asters
Carnations
Pinks
Iris
Chrysanthemums
Gladiolus
Stock
Petunia
Gaillardia
Roses
Jonquils
Calla lilies
Dahlias
Snapdragons
Cabbage leaves
Daisies
Ferns
Bird of paradise (Strelitzia)
Caladium
Calendulas
Zinnia
Larkspur
Cockscomb

Slanting Style

MATERIALS: 3 Cherry branches, 3 Photinia branches
BOWL: Grey pottery—18 × 12 × 2″

IN THIS STYLE the needlepoint holder is placed in the left front quarter of a rectangular or elliptical bowl. Choose your strongest branch and turn it so that the tips point up. This will be your Subject stem. The Secondary should be shorter and fuller than the Subject to create the illusion of weight and depth. If this stem is quite heavy, you can make it as short as ½ the length of the Subject stem. The Object should have a strong stem. The length of the Object stem will depend upon the length of the Secondary. When the Secondary is ⅔ the length of the Subject, then the Object stem is cut ½ the length. When the Secondary is ½ the length of the Subject, then the Object stem is cut ⅓ that length.

Place the Subject stem on the needlepoint holder straight up in the front left-hand corner. Now angle it forward about 70 degrees and off the left side of the bowl about 45 degrees.

Place the Secondary stem on the holder in the back left-hand corner straight up; then angle it slightly forward. Intermediaries may be necessary to fill the gap between your Subject and Secondary stems. Do not hesitate to use them. It is better to have intermediaries and thin the whole arrangement, than it is to have too sparse an effect.

The Object stem is placed to the right front of the needlepoint. Intermediaries slant back into the bowl and are shorter than the Object stem unless they follow the line of the Secondary stem.

In Slanting, as well as in the Water-Reflecting style, you are trying to recreate a bit of natural scenery. The edge of a stream with its growth coming out over the water is the setting you are creating. Water must be in evidence. As hot weather approaches, larger areas of your bowl show water. In this style of arrangement the seasons should be in evidence. In spring you would use lush spring growth; in summer you might use stiffer materials, such as reeds, cattails, iris and lilies; in the fall you might use dried branches, cattails, seed pods with small chrysanthemums, dried vines, etc.; while in the winter more dried material with forced plum and cherry blossoms, new shoots of willow, maple, aspen, narcissus would be applicable. In this latter case use anything which would suggest the coming of spring.

OUTLINE OF THE THREE MAIN STEMS WITH INTERMEDIARIES

Plant Material Suitable for the Slanting Style

Lilac
Scotch broom
Flowering trees:
- Peach
- Plum
- Cherry
- Pear
- Apple

Trees in fruit:
- Plum
- Apple
- Persimmon

Trees in new leaf
- Mountain maple
- Aspen
- Elm
- Magnolia, swamp
- Sycamore
- Mountain ash
- White birch

Trees in new leaf—*cont.*
- Cedar
- Barberry
- Huckleberry

Flowering quince
Holly
Juniper
White pine
Pitch pine
Pinyon pine
Casterbean stalks with leaves trimmed
Mountain laurel
Rhododendron
Horizontal cotoneaster
Loquat
Abelia
Ginkgo
Live oak
Split leaf philodendron
Photinia
Forsythia
Hydrangea
Asparagus fern
Lilies
Palmetto leaves
Aspidistra leaves
Hosta leaves
Tulips
Jonquils
Canna lilies
Calla lilies
Gerbera
Peonies
Zinnias
Chrysanthemums
Asters
Iris
Ferns
Aquilegia
Campanula
Roses
Snapdragons
Daisies
Caladium

Water-Reflecting Style

MATERIALS: Cherry blossoms and Grape Hyacinths
BOWL: Dark green rough pottery—18 × 12 × 2″

ALTHOUGH Slanting and Water-Reflecting styles are listed as one basic style, there are definite differences between them. Water-Reflecting arrangements should have a larger bowl than is necessary for the Slanting style. The position of the Subject stem is different and the Object can be very short, or even omitted if the illusion of a water's edge can be better represented without it.

The needlepoint holder is placed on the left front side. The Subject stem is cut from the longest branch and care is taken to find one with growth and curvature along the same side of the branch. It is placed on the needlepoint holder on the right front side, with the branch leaning out across the bowl, its tip coming out over the bowl near the right front corner.

The Secondary stem is placed to the left back of the Subject in an upright position. If there is any movement in the lines of the branch it too will lean out over the center of the bowl.

The proper measurement for the Object stem is ½ the length of the Subject, but if you have shortened the Secondary to ½, then the Object length is reduced to ⅓ that of the Subject. The Object stem is placed in the left front quarter of the needlepoint holder. In this arrangement, when you are using bare branches and short-stemmed flowers such as violets in early spring, you might arrange them as they would naturally grow without concerning yourself with the Object measurement.

As a final touch, cover the base of your work with rocks or small green growth.

Looking down into the bowl:

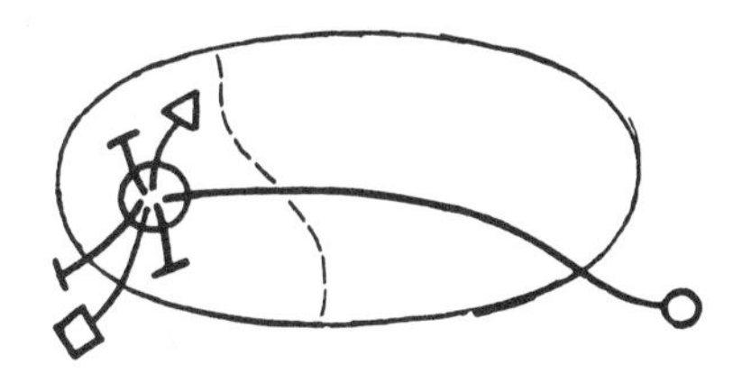

Looking across the bowl:

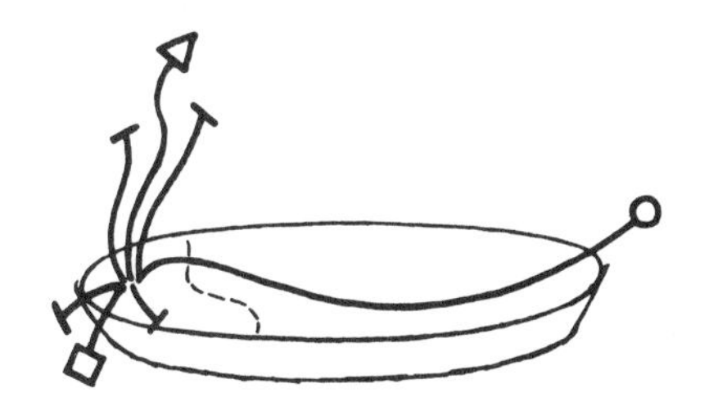

OUTLINE OF THE THREE MAIN STEMS WITH INTERMEDIARIES

Plant Material Suitable for the Water-Reflecting Style

Trees in flower:
- Apple
- Cherry
- Plum
- Peach
- Pear

Trees in fruit or seed:
- Apple
- Persimmon
- Sycamore
- Pomegranate
- Cherry

Bare branches of trees:
- Sycamore
- Elm
- Horse chestnut
- Sweet gum
- Manzanita

Magnolia, swamp
Rhododendron
Azalea
Flowering quince
Horizontal cotoneaster
Pyracantha
American larch
Violets
Roses
Iris
Lilacs
Sedum
Ferns
Santalina
Native moss
Sweet william

Small flowering bulbs:
- Anemones
- Lilies of the valley
- Crocus
- Grape hyacinth

Dried vines with berries:
- Bitter-sweet
- Virginia creeper

Cascade Style

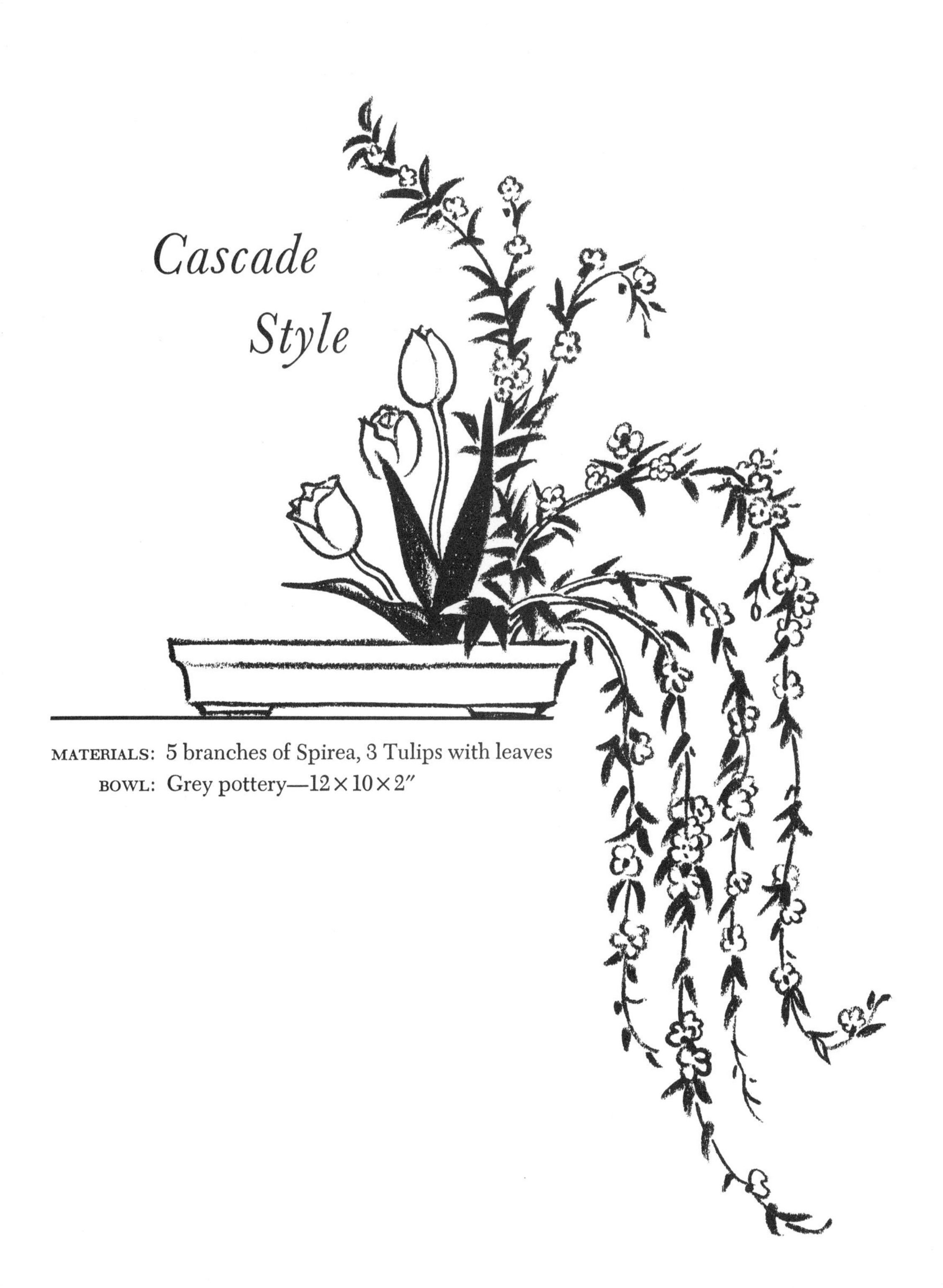

MATERIALS: 5 branches of Spirea, 3 Tulips with leaves
BOWL: Grey pottery—12 × 10 × 2″

In the Cascade style we find a natural design to suit the graceful lines of many of our shrubs, trees and vines. A few branches of spirea or wisteria together with the proper arrangement of spring flowers can recreate the charm and beauty of a spring garden within the confines of a small container.

The needlepoint holder in this style is placed in the right-hand front quarter of the bowl. It can be placed on the left-hand side should you desire to reverse the arrangement.

The Subject stem is cut at least twice the diameter of the container and is placed in the front right-hand corner of the needlepoint holder and angled forward so that it drapes over the edge of the bowl about 45 degrees to the right and forward about 120 degrees from the vertical.

The Secondary stem rises straight up in the back and any curve in the stem should flow toward the center of the bowl. This stem measures ⅔ to ½ the length of the Subject stem.

The Object stem is cut according to the measurement of the Secondary stem. If you cut the Secondary stem ⅔ of the Subject, then the Object will be cut ½ the length of the Subject stem. When the Secondary is ½ the length of the Subject, then the Object is ⅓. The Object stem is placed in the left-hand front corner of the needlepoint holder. It is put in straight down on the holder and then angled out to the left about 30 degrees and forward about 50 degrees. The intermediaries are cut shorter than the Object for the object group and are angled back into the bowl. The flowers must always face you as you work; however, the exact placement depends on the material you are using and on your personal preference.

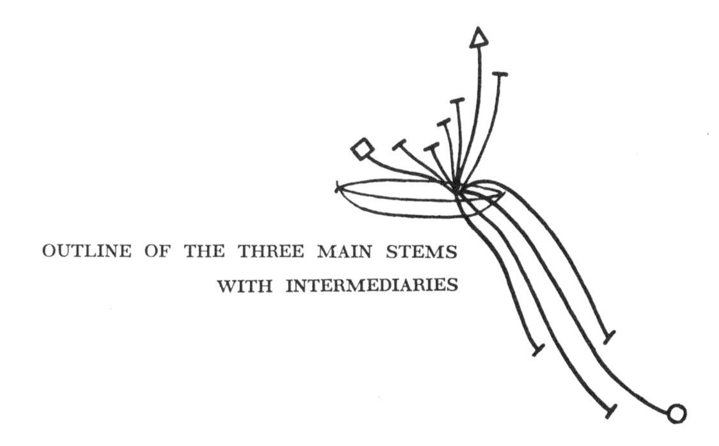

OUTLINE OF THE THREE MAIN STEMS
WITH INTERMEDIARIES

Plant Material Suitable for Cascade Style

Spirea	Silver lace vine	Petunias
Wisteria	Raspberry branches	Iris
Mimosa	Myrtle	Zinnias
Asparagus fern	Forsythia	Snapdragons
English ivy	Winter jasmine	Aquilegia
Clematis	Roses	Larkspur
Morning glory	Lilacs	Baby's breath
Grape vine	Lilies	Snowball
Perennial sweet peas	Dutch iris	Asters
Rose runners	Chrysanthemums	Campanula
Weigela		Lily of the valley

Contrasting Style

MATERIALS: Manzanita and Roses

BOWL: Black pottery, oval bowl—
12×5×2″

YOUR CHOICE of bowls for the Contrasting style will determine the size of your arrangement, but it is prettiest in a round or long, narrow bowl. A boat-shaped bowl lends itself nicely to the wide, narrow shape of the arrangement.

The needlepoint holder is placed in the center of the bowl if the bowl is round with sloping sides. When the bowl has a large, flat area, the holder must be placed as close to the front edge as possible. In the finished arrangement, all plant material must be in the front half of the bowl.

The Subject branch is cut twice the length of the bowl and is placed to the right- or left-hand side of the needlepoint holder and angled forward about 30 degrees. The Secondary branch is cut ½ the length of the Subject. It is placed on the holder opposite the Subject stem and angled forward about 30 degrees. Both the Subject and the Secondary stems are angled forward and out to opposite sides to form a forward leaning vee. The two branches should appear to be growing from the same stump as they come forward out of the container.

It is wise not to use too many intermediaries (fillers) as the object of this arrangement is to display the natural beauty of your plant material.

This is especially true when your stems are leaf-covered. When using bare branches it is permissible to use three intermediaries with the two main stems. Care must be taken to see that they are shorter than the Subject and Secondary. Intermediaries should be used only as necessary to properly finish the arrangement. I prefer two branches on the subject side with three on the shorter secondary side.

The Object group finishes the arrangement. The Object stem should be cut ⅓ the length of the Subject stem. This stem is placed in the needlepoint holder between the Subject and Secondary and angled forward about 60 degrees. The other stems of this group are cut so as to complete a pleasing arrangement.

This Contrasting style arrangement is most pleasing when it is delicate and airy, displaying the natural beauty of line. The angles of the Subject and Secondary stems can be varied to best present the material used. The lower the angles to the side and front, the taller you can place the object fillers. The higher the angle of the Subject and Secondary, the lower you place the object group.

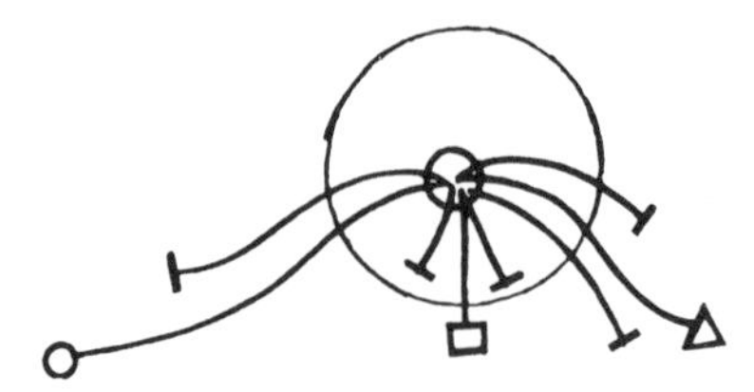

PLAN VIEW OF CONTRASTING STLYE

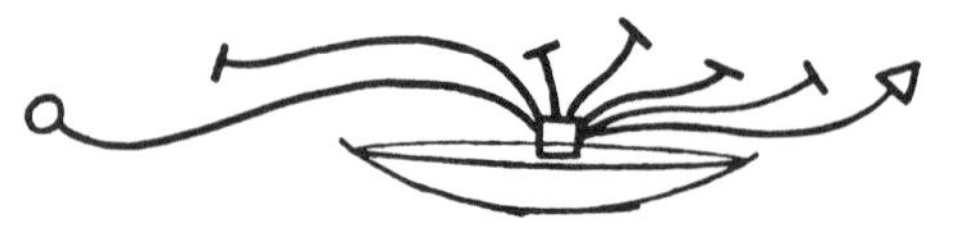

SIDE VIEW OF ARRANGEMENT

Plant Material Suitable for the Contrasting Style

Bitter-sweet
Bare line branches
Bamboo shoots
Red hot pokers
Bare branches (painted)
Pinyon pine
White pine
Wild grasses
Peeled wisteria vines
Aspidistra leaves
Driftwood
Weathered branches

Redbud branches
Flowering almond
Trees in bud or fruit:
- Sycamore
- Catalpa
- Althea
- Staghorn sumac

Bare sweet gum
Scotch broom
Weigela
Wild rose runners
Manzanita
Buddleia

Carnations
Daisies
Iris
Zinnias
Gerbera
Chrysanthemums
Roses
Tulips
Hyacinth
Gladiolus
Snapdragons
Sweet william
Balloon flower
Peonies
Verbena
Calendula

MATERIALS: 3 blue Iris buds, 8 Iris leaves
BOWL: Blue glaze—10×5×4″

Heavenly Style

THE Heavenly style is a strong line arrangement. In it the eye is drawn from the close Object group up the Secondary to the Subject stem. Stiff materials are often used for the Subject and Secondary, such as stock, Japanese iris, cattails and interesting straight branches, with pointed tips.

A round or oval bowl with sides three to five inches in height is best for the "twice the diameter" measurement of the Subject stem.

A needlepoint holder is placed in the center of the bowl regardless of its size or shape. The three main stems are placed in a straight line down the center of the holder from back to front. The Subject stem is placed toward the back of the holder, leaving room for one intermediary behind it.

The Secondary is cut ½ the length of the Subject. It is placed in front of the Subject and is angled forward about 15 degrees and to the left or right about 15 degrees.

The Object stem is cut ⅓ the length of the Subject. It is placed in front of the Secondary and is angled to the opposite side from the Secondary about 15 degrees. This stem is angled forward about 70 degrees.

When using materials such as cattails, grasses or reeds, the Subject can have one or two intermediaries to support it. These intermediaries should be cut shorter than the Subject and of varying lengths. They should be placed with one behind and one to one side of the Subject stem. This second filler should be forward as well as to one side of the Subject. There should be nothing in the arrangement to obstruct the view of the Subject stem until the Object group rises to meet it.

The Secondary can also be supported by one or two fillers. These can be placed in front of or behind the Secondary, but they must be shorter.

The Object stem will need intermediaries of the same material as the Object itself. If the material is light and airy you could use the same material as that for the Subject and Secondary intermediaries.

When making an iris arrangement in Heavenly style, using leaves as fillers, consider the grouping of three leaves as part of the main stems when used in front of the stem. The pattern for the leaves is shown on the next page.

The leaves are placed the second in front of the tallest and the lowest one in front of both of the other two, except when using only two leaves. Then the tallest one is placed in front. Groups of two leaves are added to give a naturalistic effect and sometimes to finish the front. In the Heavenly

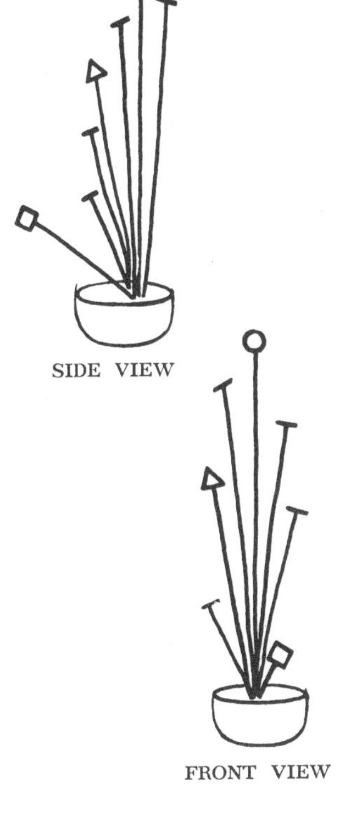

OUTLINE OF THE THREE MAIN STEMS WITH FOUR INTERMEDIARIES

style no more than two additional groups of two leaves should be used as fillers.

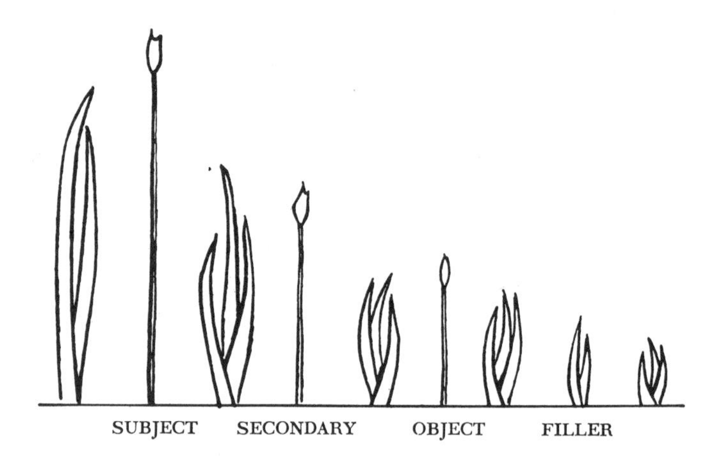

Plant Materials Suitable for the Heavenly Style

Reeds
Cattails
Wild grasses
Wheat
Yucca stems
Pampas grass
Pine thunbergi
Wisteria stems
Flowering almond
Ginger
Redbud
Purple leaf plum
Sansevieria (mother-in-law's tongue)

Onion in seed
Sea grass
Hollyhocks
Thistle
Bamboo
Delphinium
Stiff grape vine
Stiff wisteria in bloom
Amaryllis
Gladiolus
Sweet peas (massed)
Sweet william

Oriental poppies
Bellflower
Larkspur
Iris
Gerbera
Petunias
Chrysanthemums
Lilies
Roses
Asparagus fern
Cockscomb
Begonia
Dahlia
Geranium with foliage

Narcissus— Naturalistic Arrangement

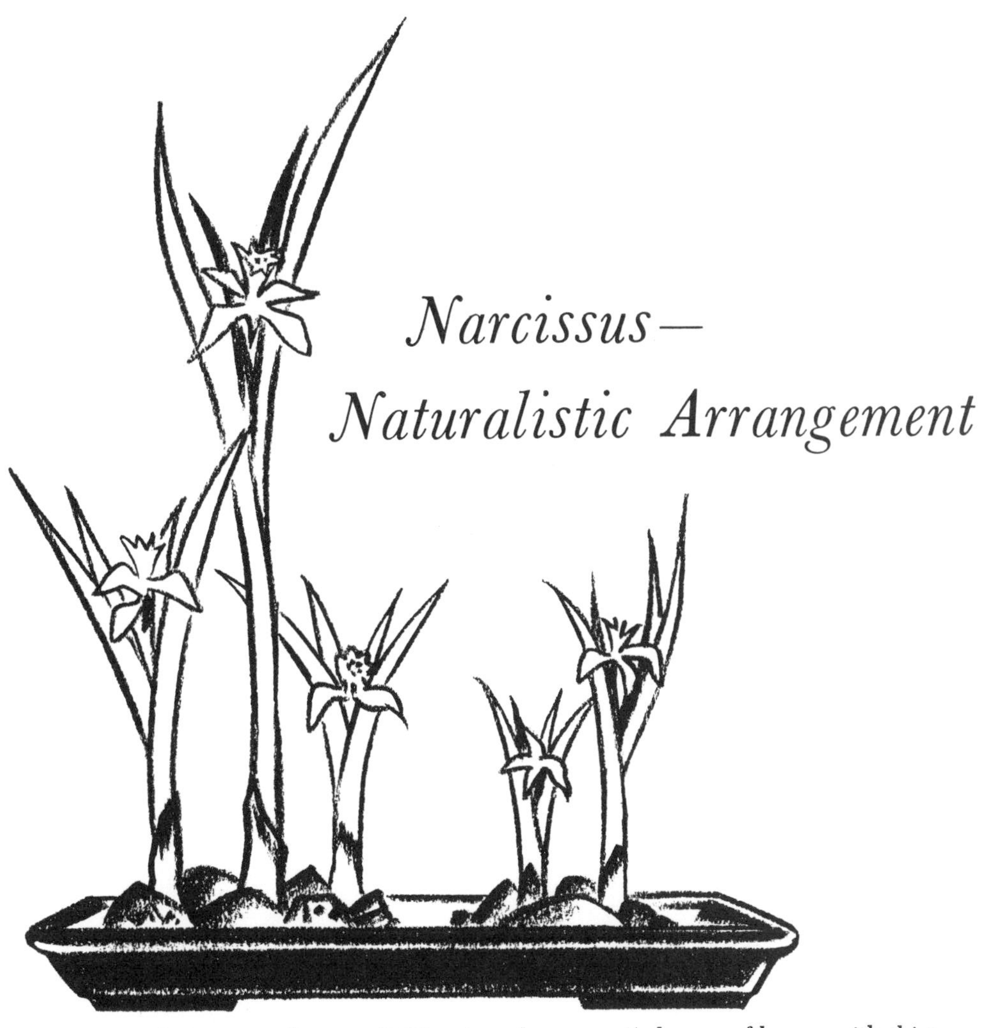

MATERIALS: 5 Narcissus flowers, 20 Narcissus leaves or 5 clumps of leaves with skirt

BOWL: Black—18 × 12 × 2″; rocks to cover holders and 4 needlepoint holders

THE Japanese use narcissus in many of their winter arrangements, both alone and with other plant material. Narcissus is thought of as the plant of the two seasons, as its growth spans both winter and spring months. A combination of narcissus and dried plant material of the previous season suggests past, present and future. Pine used with narcissus leads one to speculate on the eternal and the temporal, as pine expresses the eternal while the narcissus denotes new life. A group of three or five blossoms of narcissus with their own leaves suggests the passing of winter and the hope and joy of spring. This naturalistic arrangement displays the flower in simple loveliness and elegance.

The techniques used in handling narcissus were designed to beautify it in the small confines of the *suiban* or low Moribana type bowl.

The Japanese use field-grown plants as they usually are hardier than greenhouse plants; however, the limitations of potted, forced plants are not so great that we cannot use them. Our greatest problem will be in the frailty of the skirt which binds the plant together. If you cannot handle the skirt without tearing it, use floral tape to bind the leaves and head together provided it does not show in the finished arrangement.

To make a naturalistic narcissus arrangement, one needs a large flat bowl, three to five needlepoint holders, a pot of five or six flowering narcissus, clay, rocks or small plant material for covering the needlepoint holders. The following are suggested for assembling the arrangement.

1. Cut the narcissus clump (leaves and flower) close to the bulb, being careful to cut at least one inch of the skirt at the bottom with the stalk. Cut five or six clumps of flowers with their leaves. (One or two of the flowers should be in bud.) Try to graduate the size of the leaves of the clumps as they are cut.

2. Put all of the leaves and flowers in a pitcher of deep cool water and place in a cool spot for three to four hours. This will harden and strengthen them, and make them last longer.

3. Choose a large flat bowl—elliptical or rectangular—about 12 × 18″, with shallow sides, to hold the arrangement. Neutral colors or black are best.

4. Arrange the needlepoint holders in the bottom as diagrammed. Small holders will hold the slender stems, but if you do not have five small holders use two medium-sized ones and one small one. There must be space between the flowers so that each clump will be in clear view.

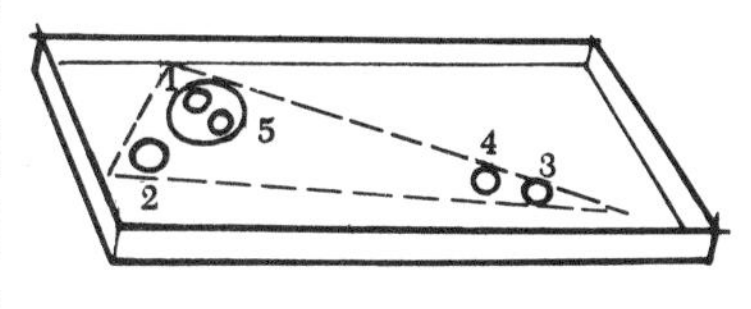

5. If you plan to move the finished arrangement, it is wise to anchor each needlepoint holder with floral clay.

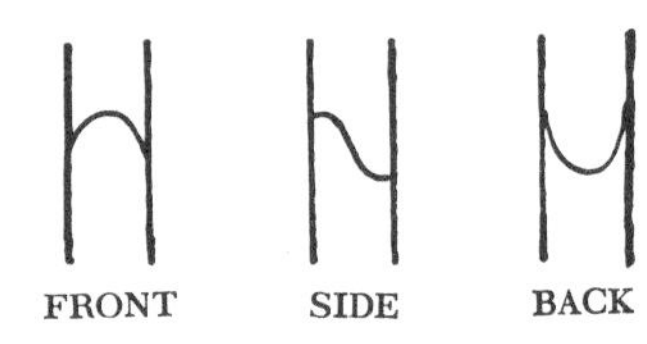

6. Observe the thin skirt which encircles the leaves and flower.

7. Remove the skirt from the base of the plant by rolling it gently on the edge of the table with a slight pressure of the side of your hand. When the skirt is free, gently work it off the stalk and lay it, the leaves and the flower, to one side, being careful not to tear the skirt.

8. Repeat this operation until all clumps have been separated.

9. Now you are ready to assemble five groups of four leaves and one flower each. The finished groups should be different in height.

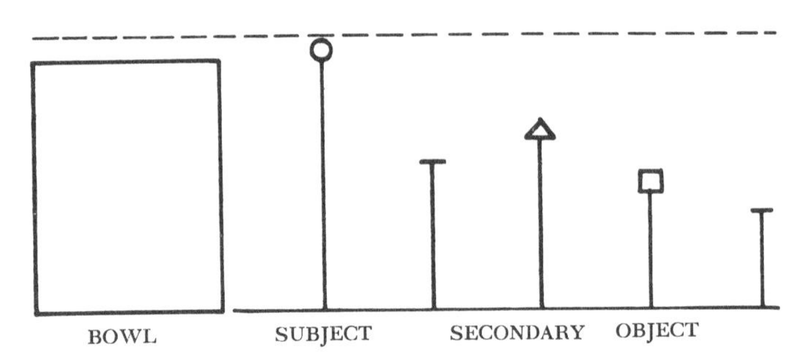

10. The tallest leaf, which measures the length of the bowl, serves as a measure for all the other leaves. It is a part of group 1. Now choose three other leaves, each progressively one inch shorter than the first one, and a flower. They should look like this:

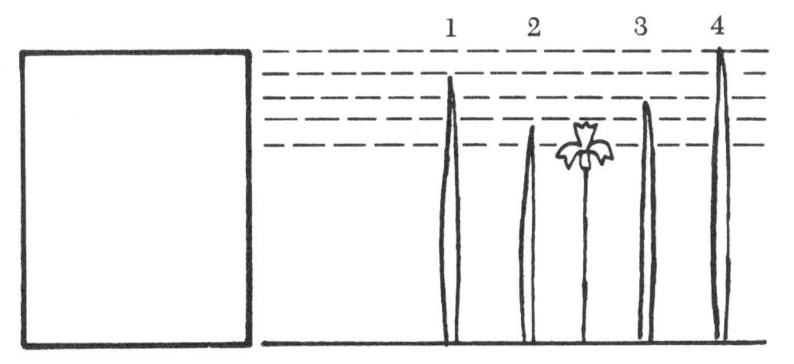

11. Following the same procedure, select four leaves and a flower for your group 2. The tallest leaf should be ⅔ the height of the leaf in group 1.

12. Group 3 is made in the same manner, but with the tallest leaf measuring ½ the tallest leaf in group 1.

13. Now make two smaller groups of four leaves and a bud each to use as fillers.

14. Now you have before you five groups of leaves and flowers, all of different heights. They should look like this:

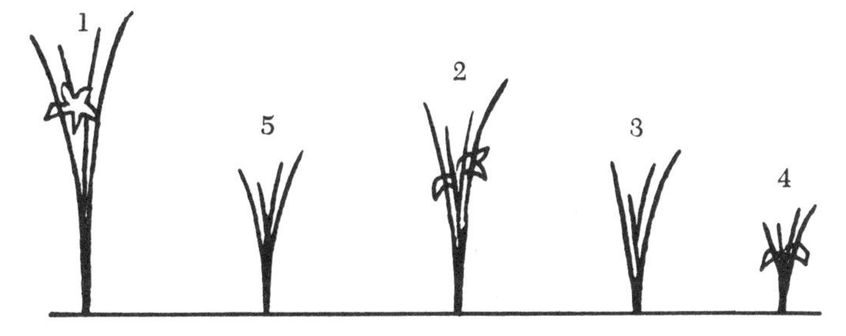

15. Now you are ready to reassemble the leaves and flowers. Line them up as diagrammed

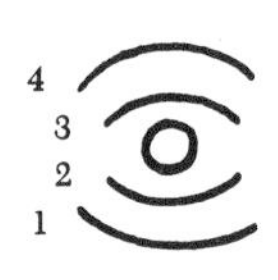

in number 10. Cut each leaf about one inch shorter than the last. Assemble the leaves starting with 1 and 2 facing 3 and 4. Cut the bottom at an angle and insert in the skirt. Make certain that the high curve of the skirt is in front of leaf number 1. Pick up the flower, turning the brown skin which covered the bloom to the back. Insert the stem between leaves 2 and 3, with the flower facing leaf number 1.

16. Repeat until all five groups have been assembled. Number them as diagrammed and place on needlepoint holders having corresponding numbers.

17. When all of the plants are in place, cover the base of your work with one or two inches of sprigs of moss, santalina, or similar material. If this is unobtainable, use rocks in a naturalistic manner.

18. Spray the whole arrangement with a fine mist of water to freshen it and then put it in its final location.

19. Add water.

Iris — Naturalistic Arrangement

MATERIALS: 5 Iris buds, approximately 35 leaves
BOWL: Oval black pottery—12 × 18 × 2″

The iris is a natural choice for arrangements celebrating Boy's Day on May 5, one of Japan's national festivals, as it is the symbol of strength and virility, and begins to show its lovely colors early in May.

During the months of May and June, iris arrangements abound, both at home and in exhibitions. The variety of design and combinations of irises with other plant materials is almost limitless. In the more classical designs irises are used alone. In modern designs we find them used with reeds, lotus, driftwood, other flowers, shells, baskets, stone and new green shoots of water-loving trees and shrubs. Since the iris has always been at home in Japan, many of the schools have evolved their own rules for displaying the iris to best show its natural growth.

The Ohara School has developed its "natural scenery" type of arrangement for iris along the same lines as that of the narcissus. However, it should be noted that the Japanese iris is a large flower on a very long stalk and the leaves are much longer and thinner than the American variety. With this in mind, we must realize that our arrangements are apt to look heavy unless we choose our leaves and flowers with care; or else scale down the whole arrangement. We can use smaller bowls and perhaps three flowers instead of the traditional five, and even omit one or two groups of leaves. This would be quite permissible in a variation of the basic style.

In order to make the traditional arrangement, one needs:

1. A large rectangular or oval bowl with a flat bottom.

2. Four needlepoint holders.

3. Five iris buds with stalks.

4. Forty to fifty leaves of various sizes. Cut more than you expect to use so that you will have enough to match the "hooks" on the end of each leaf.

5. Rocks to cover the base of your work.

After you have gathered your materials, put your iris and leaves to soak in cool, deep water for several hours. The longer they harden, the firmer they will be to handle when you make the arrangement.

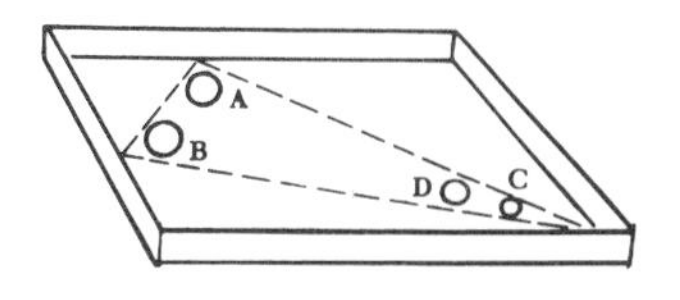

Follow the diagram at the right in placing your needlepoint holders in the bottom of the container. If you plan to move the arrangement, use clay to anchor the holders in place. Make certain holders A and B are heavy enough to hold the long stems and leaves and the needles are long enough to grip without splitting the stems.

When your holders are in place, lay the iris and leaves out on paper and work with a minimum of handling.

The tallest iris flower should be twice the length of the bowl when using Japanese iris; but for American iris I suggest you choose the longest and strongest stem, making certain that it is not shorter than the length plus the depth of the bowl.

The tallest iris is the Subject (1) and is the basic length for all measurements. The Secondary iris (3) should be ⅔, and the Object (2) should be ½ the length of the Subject stem. Flowers (4 and 5) are fillers and should be tight buds.

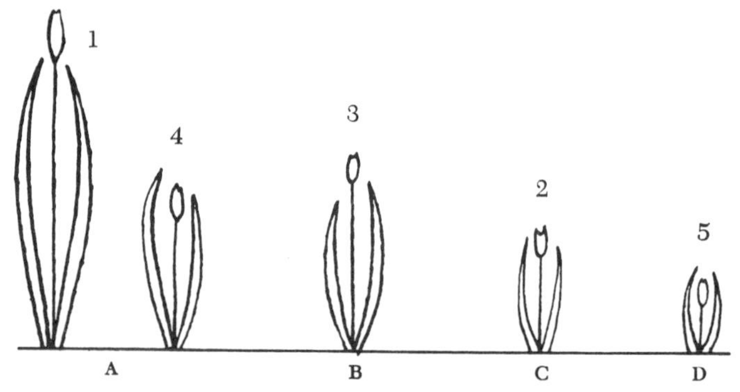

A — the Subject and Filler which go on A holder.

B — the Secondary flower which goes on B holder.

C — the Object flower which goes on C holder.

D — the Filler for the Object which goes on the D holder.

As the American iris tends to make more than one flower on a stalk, it is recommended that you remove all buds except the one you need. Clean the stalk as well as possible and try to hide the scar behind the leaves.

Having set aside your five flowers, you are now ready to assemble the leaves. There are three groups of leaves for each of the main stems: two groups of two leaves and one group of three leaves. The tallest leaf for your Subject stem should be about 3 inches shorter than the flower. The second leaf in this group should be about 1½ inches shorter than the first. The tallest leaf in the second group should be about 2 inches shorter than the tallest leaf in the first group, with the second leaf in this group about 1½ inches shorter than this. The third group of leaves consists of three with the center leaf about 2 inches shorter than the tallest leaf in the second group. The other two leaves of this third group are graduated down 1½ inches.

The Secondary group of leaves are assembled in the same way as the Subject groups.

In order to indicate young growth, the tallest leaf is about 1 inch taller than the flower in the Object group. The spaces between the leaves in this group can also be shorter. The sketches on the following page should help in assembling the various groups of leaves. Notice the little "hooks" on the end of each leaf. Make sure that it is reversed as in the sketches. Start with the tallest leaf facing right with the second leaf facing to the left. The next leaf faces left while the second leaf in this group faces to the right, and so forth. Follow down in order under each of the Groups A, B, etc., as shown on the following page. Also, when assembling groups of two leaves, always see that the longest leaf crosses in front of the shortest at the base. In groups of three leaves, the shortest leaf always crosses in front of the other two.

The groups opposite are lined up as they are to be placed on the holders, starting from the back and working forward. The flowers are placed between the groups of leaves as indicated.

Fillers repeat the "hook" of the main branch they support.

In case your leaves are not as strong as you would like them to be, leave a little room at the back of your holder so that you can brace the leaves with a piece of iris stem. Place flowers as close to the base of the leaves as possible and in

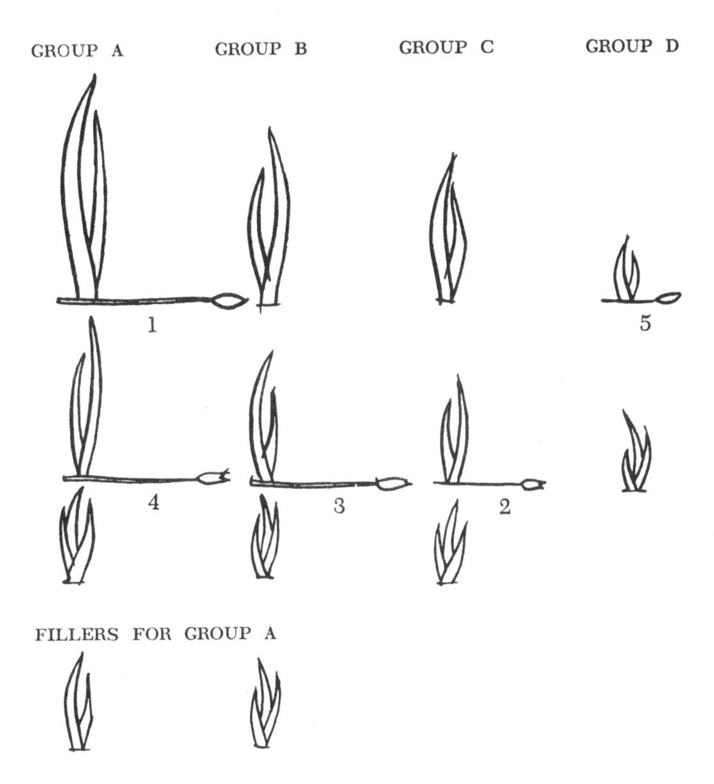

such a way as to have them appear to be growing up between the leaves. It is important that the flowers have plenty of room to open. When you have placed the first two groups of leaves and flowers, add the shorter group of three leaves in front to finish the group. A has two groups of filler leaves which should be placed inside the triangle on A holder. Continue placing Groups B, C and D.

To complete your arrangement add rocks to cover the needlepoint holders.

Some schools refer to this arrangement as the "fish-path" as there are spaces between the rocks and iris for fish to swim through. This arrangement is greatly admired by the Japanese in hot weather as they can imagine the coolness of a lakeside while viewing it.

In spring the iris leaves are cut taller than the buds. In summer the flower head is taller than the accompanying leaves. Iris seed pods are added to the arrangement in the fall to increase the seasonal effect.

MATERIALS: 2 Water Lilies
8 Water Lily pads
2 groups wild grasses

BOWL: Elliptical white pottery—
15×24×2″

Summer Water Arrangement

UNTIL recently the Japanese used lotus blossoms or pond lilies almost exclusively in Buddhist ceremonies. Today, however, they have developed a summer arrangement of lotus blossoms which, combined with other materials in a large container, expresses the quiet coolness and serenity of a summer lake or pond. It is this arrangement we will work on in this lesson.

In placing the lilies and lily pads in a summer arrangement think of them as the Object group and fillers for the Subject and Secondary branches. The Subject and Secondary stems can be chosen according to the dictates of seasons and locale; however, they must be plant material which grows near water.

In the spring, you may use three irises with ten to thirteen leaves for your Subject and Secondary groups. Place them as you would in a Traditional Iris Arrangement. The lilies and lily pads will form the Object group and finish the arrangement. Willow and spirea branches lend themselves to Slanting style placement of the Subject and Secondary branches.

In the summer, reeds, cattails, arrowroot, calla lilies with their own leaves, and similar types of plants make interesting Subject and Secondary groups when used in an Upright style with the lilies and lily pads.

In the fall, colorful shrubs and tree branches with driftwood, or bamboo with dried marsh grasses, lend poignancy to the arrangement and represent the approach of winter.

In the winter, lotus pods may be used in more modern types of arrangement.

The following materials are needed to make the Summer Water arrangement:

A large flat container. It should be about 16 × 20 × 2″ to show off the lily pads properly.

Two clumps of reeds, wild grasses, cattails with their own blades, or similar types of material.

Floral tape or wire for binding the reeds together at the base.

Two holders, one medium-sized and one small. Either the needlepoint or the Japanese lead Shippo type are permissible.

Floral clay for anchoring the holders.

Two lotus blossoms or pond lilies; one in bud, the other in full bloom. Cut them with 5-inch stems.

The rule is at least two open pads to each flower. Six to eight lily pads of various sizes and stems. Have at least two open leaves with 6-inch stems and two leaves in tight curl. Keep the lilies and pads moist at all times.

Two toothpicks or short sticks for anchoring the curled leaves.

Syringe for forcing water or a weak solution of lead acetate into the stems.

Once you have gathered your materials, you are ready to make the arrangement.

It will be necessary to work fast so that the lilies and lily pads do not have a chance to dry out. If possible, lay them in a large bowl and keep covered with water until you are ready to use them. This will aid you in seeing the natural lines in the pads and help you to choose the right pad for each position.

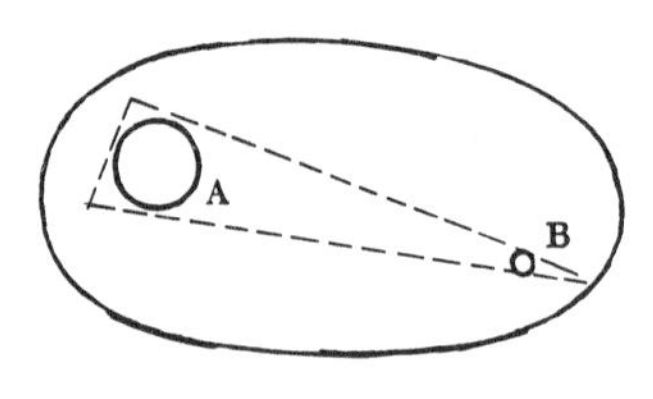

1. Anchor in position the two needlepoint holders A and B in the bowl as shown in the diagram.

2. Sort your reeds into two groups. Use the strongest ones in your Subject group and the others in the Secondary group. Measure them as for an Upright arrangement. The Subject is best if measured the length plus the depth of the container when your material is heavy. If it is light and has strong lines, then use the one and one-half plus the depth of your bowl measurement. The Secondary group is cut ⅔ the length of the Subject. Make sure that the lengths are staggered to create a naturalistic effect. Wrap floral tape around the base of the reeds to hold them firm. It should not show in the finished arrangement.

3. Place the Subject and Secondary groups on holder A as you would for the basic Upright style. The Subject group will go straight up on the back of the holder and angle slightly back. The Secondary group will be placed in front of the Subject on holder A and will angle out toward the side of the container about 30 degrees and forward about 45 degrees.

4. Be sure that your work is tight at the base and flares at the top.

5. To finish the group on holder A you will use one lily and four lily pads. One leaf should be in tight curl while the other three are graduated in size.

a. Cut the stem of the lily bud about 4 inches long and place close to the base of the Subject and Secondary stems facing toward the center of the bowl. Take the largest leaf and place it close to the Subject and Secondary stems on the outside of the group. The second leaf is cut short and placed forward on the holder to cover it. The third leaf is left with a long stem and is anchored on the holder so it will float toward the center of the bowl.

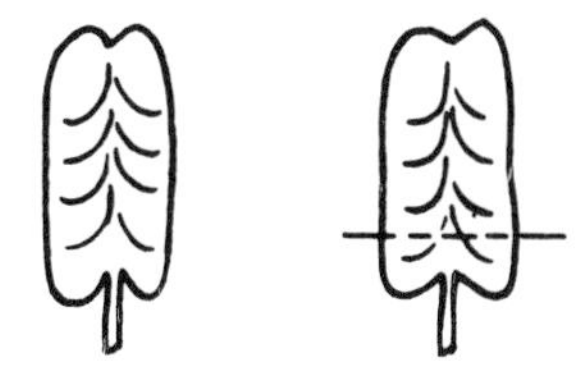
HOW TO CUT THE LILY PAD

b. The fourth leaf is the tight one. It is cut across the bottom so that it will stand up straight. A toothpick is stuck through the two

TOOTHPICK

sides and it is stood up behind the third leaf and anchored under the holder or through the clay. It should be clearly in view.

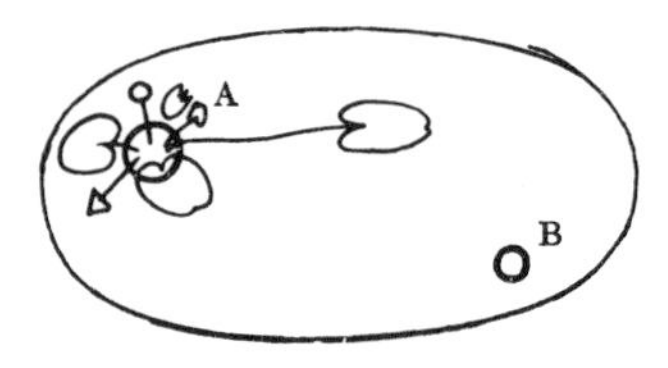

6. When your work on holder A is completed, it should look like the diagram when looking down into the bowl.

7. Holder B will hold the Object group of one lily and four lily pads. Cut the second lily blossom about 2 inches long and stand it up on the center of the holder. Cut the stem of the largest lily pad about 3 inches and stand it up so that it curves out over the edge of the bowl. Take the second largest leaf and cut the stem short and place it over the holder so that it covers it. The split in the pad should fit around the stem of the flower. The stem of the third pad is left several inches long. Anchor it on holder under second pad. It is left free to float toward the center of the bowl and the other floating pad, or across the bowl and parallel with the other leaf. The fourth tight leaf is cut, fastened through with a toothpick and placed to the right of the group on holder B in back of the first lily pad. It must stand straight up.

PLAN VIEW

8. Fill the bowl with water if you have worked with it dry. Adjust the lily pads and your arrangement is complete. Check your placement against the diagram on the next page.

When reeds are used in summer for the Subject and Secondary groups, you may want to bend two or three reeds to indicate movement and life on the pond. It is wise to test your material before you make the arrangement to determine how easily it breaks. Then make the arrangement and bend the reeds as a finishing touch. Do not bend them at random, which would only create confusion. Bend two or three reeds toward or away from the center of the bowl.

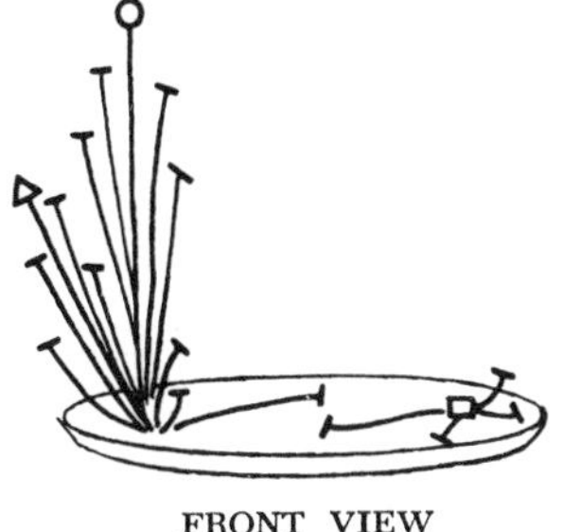

FRONT VIEW

In the fall, when using wild marsh grasses, it is natural that the effect at the base of your work should seem cluttered. Some confusion at this time will emphasize the approach of wind and weather.

The Japanese often place whole lily pads out of the water. Before we attempt this we must bear in mind our lack of humidity and be prepared to spray the pads often. It is also wise to force water into the stems of the pads and lilies. This will tend to extend the life and beauty of the plants.

Japanese Pot-Pourri

Making a Japanese arrangement from words and illustrations without some understanding of the Japanese mentality compares with making a pot-pourri without using spices. It is the spice which combines the fragrance and creates a new whole. So it is with Ikebana. The spices of Ikebana are the subtleties of thought, the suggestions of ideas, the symbolism, a love of nature in all its manifestations, an appreciation of clean line and a long history of myths and folklore. In this chapter I would like to list a few of the spices as they pertain to flower arranging.

The Japanese consider flowers as acceptable an art medium as stone, paint, wood or metals. The Japanese thought on flower arranging seems to be, "Why shouldn't we consider Ikebana an art form? Has it not continued throughout all our history to add beauty to our lives? Have Greece and Rome perpetuated their ancient arts?" Flower arranging, because of its eternal applicability, is as expressive today as it has been down through the years.

Purpose is one of the keys to understanding Ikebana. The Japanese are a people who love the living present, but who also love to be surrounded by objects which suggest permanence and unchanging ideas. In their arrangements grass and pine are not incompatible, as these two materials suggest the temporal and the eternal at one and the same time. The practiced arranger will always try to express a spiritual or mental concept in the arrangement.

Flowers of a poisonous nature are never used.

Flowers keep longer when they are not crowded.

The flowers which last the longest when cut are most admired. Flowers with a short life are not often used.

Legend suggests that flowers have souls not unlike humans. Exhibitions are not competitive. How can one judge the soul of a flower?

An arrangement is the expression of the individuality of the arranger, and the life rhythm is more important than proportion.

Seika and Shôka are synonymous. They are the formalized styles of the Ikenobo School.

Nandina is often used in the house after one has had a nightmare. The presence of this flower is supposed to ward off a repeat occurrence.

The Japanese do not mix flowers with trees and shrubs in their gardens. Some people have cutting gardens for their flowers, but most flowers are bought from florist shops. Buds and semi-opened flowers are preferred, as one of the joys of the finished arrangement is to watch the blossoms unfold. Also there is less likelihood of damaging the tender petals between the shop and home.

A piece of rice paper is wrapped carefully around the blossoms of flowers with large heads such as chrysanthemums, lilies, roses and tulips. (We could use tissues.) This is done to prevent damage to the bloom and it also holds it in the bud stage until it is used in an arrangement.

Seasons

Winter. At this time of the year plant materials are sparse, flowers few. Bare branches and pine arrangements are light and delicate. Driftwood with a few blossoms can be used. No water is allowed to show. Heika is most suited for winter arrangements.

Spring. Now the young green branches are used to make variegated green arrangements. Jonquils and narcissus are used with ferns. Again, arrangements are light and delicate. Some water can be allowed to show.

Summer. For this season both branches and flowers are more densely massed. A large expanse of water can be shown. Iris and lotus are popular. Fresh reeds and water plants are used abundantly.

Fall. Now the expanse of water becomes smaller again and leafy branches are used with fewer flowers. Dried flowers, seed pods, etc., are added to the fresh plant material. There is a strong use of the dried grasses and reeds which grow along the rice paddies and streams to emphasize the coming winter.

Garden influences become increasingly important and useful as we gain a more naturalistic approach to arrangements. False perspective in the garden can be attained by placing a tall tree in front of a shorter one. A lantern half hidden behind a tall tree gives the illusion of depth or distance. Sometimes several groups of plantings are united through the use of odd objects (tomes). These tomes are placed so that they seem to be a part of each grouping. These odd additions are called center objects. They may be stones, lanterns, specimen plants or walks; anything which will catch and focus the eye. We can use these illusionary practices also in arrangement.

Stones

Stones can be used throughout the year to cover the needlepoint holder in Moribana arrangements. Usually you will use small stones of ½ inch diameter, and all of the same color. Different-colored stones denote the seasons.

Green stones are used in spring to create illusion of new growth.

White stones are used in summer because they create a cooling effect.

Red stones are used in fall and match the glorious autumn foliage.

Black stones are used in winter as they represent the dormant earth.

Don't be limited by commercially packed stones. Your summer holidays can turn up black lava, crystals, broken bits of glass and natural obsidian. Shells from the beach add an interesting note to summer arrangements. Even the coal bin will inspire one to collect bits of glassy black which can be cleaned and added to winter and early spring arrangements, while the furnace will offer red clinkers with rough texture simulating the high crags of Japan.

Symbols

The Asiatics have always recognized the natural and spiritual worlds in their religions. The Hindus have their Brahman and all the attendant gods and goddesses; the Japanese their combination of Shinto and Buddhism. Shinto unites man with the natural world while Buddhism lifts him to the world of Spirit through prayer and meditation. Aside from Buddha there are a host of lesser beings who intercede along with the spirits of the ancestors. The symbols are many. There is Buddha sitting on a lotus blossom as though he had risen from the water, while Amida, the god of mercy, holds his hand out in benediction.

Jung says that our own Christianity is based on the same archtypes or symbols. We have Christ representing the union between Heaven and Earth (the Virgin Mary), in comparison:

Japanese —	Heaven	Man	Earth
Christian —	God	Christ	Mary
	Spirit	Man	Earth

THE SYMBOLISM OF FLOWERS

Willow Branches and Camellia — suggest a young girl dressed in her gaily colored kimono.

Narcissus — a flower of two seasons, winter and spring. They represent strength, courage devotion and hope.

Peach — symbol of life. Feminine qualities of gentleness and mildness.

Lotus — symbol of Buddhism and also used for funeral arrangements. It is a symbol of life and immortality. Meditation.

Lily — represents respect and purity.

Pine — symbol of eternal life. Suggests tranquility, faithfulness and integrity. The pine with twin needles is used in weddings as it represents long life; but if one of the pair of needles dies, both die.

Chrysanthemum — strength, courage and dignity. Encouragement to struggle. In the nineteenth century it was made the exclusive symbol of the emperor.

Iris (and its sword-like leaves) — virility, boldness and power.

Bamboo — faithfulness, flexibility, strength and endurance.

Cherry Blossoms — virtues of loyalty and filial love. They are likened to the Samurai who spends his life preparing for the battle in which he is killed in a few days.

Evergreens — constancy, unchanging life rhythm.

Plum Blossoms — symbol of good fortune.

Pine and Bamboo — used together at New Year's Festival, they represent propriety and good luck.

Climbing Vines (such as hardy sweet peas, ivy and clematis and morning glory) — represent affection.

Willow Branches — denote perseverance.

Azalea — symbol of family devotion, as the blossoms lie very close to the parent stem.

Peony — the flower of happiness and prosperity.

Pine and Rose — as a combination they reflect the Japanese love of contrast. Pine is masculine, bold and vital, while the rose is feminine, colorful and fragile. The combination stimulates the imagination to the conflict of opposites in human relations of life and love.

Festivals

Just as we have national holidays based on religious and historical events, the Japanese have theirs. However, the Japanese holidays have lost much of their religious significance in antiquity and are thought of today as festivals.

Today there are five principal festivals celebrated in the Japanese calendar year. They are anticipated by all the people. In a land where people are accustomed to privation and hard work, the festival becomes an occasion for social gregariousness, gaiety and the pursuit of pleasure.

The five festivals fall on odd days of the odd months—a carry-over of the Chinese philosophical concept that "all even numbers are feminine while the odd numbers are masculine." The New Year's Festival begins on the first day of the new year and ends on January 7. The last day of the Festival is celebrated by drinking a medicinal sake which is supposed to give good health throughout the coming year. March 3 commemorates Girl's Day; May 5 is Boy's Day. The seventh of July revives the myth of the Star Festival, while the ninth of September is the Festival of Chrysanthemums.

Arrangements for the Festivals

The New Year's Festival calls for a traditional arrangement of pine, bamboo, orchid and chrysanthemum. This combination has been named the "Four Cultured Gentlemen" because of the symbolism attached to the plants. This arrangement is placed in the Tokonoma. Outside at the gate entrance of the house one finds another arrangement of pine and bamboo. Both rough- and smooth-barked pine boughs, which indicate male and female properties, are used with stalks of bamboo placed behind them—an arrangement is placed on either side of the gate. Overhead is hung a fringed rope of straw with small strips of rectangular white paper hanging down. The symbolic significance of these arrangements is buried in the nature-loving Shinto faith.

The Girl's Day Festival, on the third of March, is honored with arrangements of peach blossoms. Sometimes the peach blossoms are complemented with the small yellow flowers of wild mustard. These arrangements are made in many styles, but those used to accompany the doll collection are usually in the Heika and Seika forms.

Boy's Day is held on the fifth of May. An arrangement of iris seems most fitting to commemorate this day, as both the sword-like leaves and the flower of the iris on its tall stalk symbolize strength and virility. Irises have been arranged simply so as to display their natural characteristics and, on this day, traditional arrangements are most satisfying.

The Star Festival on the seventh of July commemorates the myth concerning lovers who were separated and can only meet on this day of the year in the sky across the Milky Way. Arrangements of bamboo are used in the home, while street decorations consist of whole bamboo trees lining the sidewalks and from which are displayed colored strips of paper that twist and flutter in the breezes.

The Chrysanthemum Festival is held on the ninth of September. It honors the emblem of the Emperor and the national flower of Japan. Potted plants which have been nurtured and shaped throughout the year are exhibited all over the country. Tokyo has a special exhibit of chrysanthemums in every conceivable size and shape. Home arrangements are made of the beautiful and hardy flower.

There are many other national as well as individual days of celebration, and many of these have traditional arrangements to accompany ancient ritual. They add joy and a sense of community to otherwise limited and monotonous lives.

Calendar of Flowers

January	Pine	July	Morning glory
February	Plum	August	Lotus
March	Peach and Pear	September	"The Seven Grasses"
April	Cherry		
May	Azalea, Peony and Wisteria	October	Chrysanthemum
		November	Maples
June	Iris	December	Camellia

Bibliography

Houn Ohara. *Everyone's Flower Arrangement.* Tokyo, Japan: Ryufusha Publishing Co., Ltd., 1957.

Houn Ohara. *Flower Arrangements of the Ohara School.* Kyoto, Japan: Mitsubana and Co.

Ikebana International Magazine. Tokyo, Japan: Dai Nippon Printing Co., Ltd.

Ohara Center Magazine. Ohara Center, Tokyo, Japan.

Oshikawa, J. and H. H. Gorham. *Manual of Japanese Flower Arrangement.*

Rachel E. Carr. *Steppingstones to Japanese Floral Art.*

Sofu Teshigawara. *Colored Pictures of Representative Flower Arrangements.* Tokyo, Japan: Ryufusha Publishing Co., Ltd., 1956.

Sofu Teshigawara. *Ikebana.* Tokyo, Japan: Sogetsukai, Publisher, 1952.

Sofu Teshigawara. *Modern Japanese Art of Flower Arrangements.* Kohata, Japan: Hanao-Shiori-Sha, Publisher.

The books listed above are available through the Charles E. Tuttle Company, Rutland, Vermont.

Tatsuo Ishimoto. *The Art of Plant and Driftwood Arrangement.* Crown Publishers, Inc., 1954.

Seiko Hara. *Flowers Around the Clock.* David McKay Company.

Sofu Teshigawara. *Ikebana, Japanese Flower Arrangements.* Studio Publications, 1958.

Lida Webb. *Popular Styles of Japanese Flower Arrangement.* Hearthside Press, 1959.

Betty Pettit. *Plants for Albuquerque Gardens.* Southwest Printing Co.

Ellen G. Allen. *Japanese Flower Arrangement.* National Council Books, Inc., Phila., Publishers.

G. B. Sansom. *Japan, A Short Cultural History.* D. Appleton Century Company, Inc.

Donald Keene. *Living Japan.*

Issotii Nishikawa. *Floral Art of Japan.* Tourist Library, Vol. I.

Mary Cokely Wood. *Flower Arrangement of Japan.* Tuttle.

H. S. K. Yamaguchi. *We Japanese.* Fujiya Hotel.

Mumsterberg. *The Folk Arts of Japan.* Tuttle.